HOW TO
LAUGH IN IRONIC
AMUSEMENT
DURING YOUR
EXISTENTIAL CRISIS

POEMS + MEMES

JAMES MCCRAE

**THOUGHT
CATALOG**
Books

THOUGHTCATALOG.COM
NEW YORK · LOS ANGELES

```
THOUGHT
CATALOG
Books
```

Copyright © 2021 James McCrae.
All rights reserved.

Published by Thought Catalog Books, an imprint of the digital magazine Thought Catalog, which is owned and operated by The Thought & Expression Company LLC, an independent media organization based in Brooklyn, New York and Los Angeles, California.

This book was produced by Chris Lavergne and Noelle Beams. Designed by KJ Parish. Special thanks to Brianna Wiest for creative editorial direction and Isidoros Karamitopoulos for circulation management.

Visit us at thoughtcatalog.com and shopcatalog.com.

Made in the United States of America.

ISBN 978-1-949759-40-2

All poems and art created between late
2019 and early 2021 in New York City, Los
Angeles, Austin, and Mexico.

"WHILE LOOKING FOR THE LIGHT YOU MAY SUDDENLY BE DEVOURED BY THE DARKNESS AND FIND THE TRUE LIGHT."

– JACK KEROUAC

ALL TOO HUMAN

I woke up inside a human body and now I can't remember who I'm supposed to be.

checks ID

I have a name, a social security number, an occupation, a bank account, but it feels like I'm forgetting something. For example, how did I get here? And why am I currently crying on the floor in a state of subtle terror?

My human avatar is nice enough. The fractal high-fidelity biological craftsmanship shows impressive signs of higher intelligence. So why do I feel the nagging need to rip off my skin and merge with the great mirage?

Some god or advanced AI hiding behind the simulation curtain must certainly have a sense of humor.

Am I stuck inside a cage? Or is this seemingly stable 3D stage merely a shadow artifact cast by the light of higher mind?

scans hyperspace for an answer: none found

What sort of unsupervised science experiment is this? I demand to speak to the manager. Or the aliens.

Maybe I slipped and fell into the wrong dimension.

Can I outsource my thoughts? My brain only gets me into trouble. Maybe I should start microdosing mushrooms. Or get a life coach. Or a lobotomy. The more answers I seek the more questions I find.

How strange it is to be anything at all.

I could have sworn there was something important I'm supposed to be doing, but now it escapes me. The meaning of life is a hard mantra to memorize.

Did my soul incarnate on a sacred mission or am I trapped inside the spinning wheel of karma? Am I part of the inside joke or am I the punchline? Either way I'm not getting the joke. Maybe I need a better sense of humor.

Oh well. I guess I'll sit down in the sunlight and enjoy the sensation of breath in my lungs and grass between my toes, here on this living planet, halfway between the jungle and the stars.

I feel strange.

You're standing on a spinning rock in outer space for a fleeting moment before your body dissipates into the ether.

Literally what is normal?

The homesick
alien in me
recognizes
the homesick
alien in you.

OPEN

What I want is to open up,
to merge my body
with the energy vortex around me,
to clean my subconscious closet
and burn the clutter in ritual,
to open my vocal chords
and hear the universe expanding,
to inject my veins with sunlight
and bask in my aura's glow,
to become my breath
and exhale myself into Times Square
and wait for strangers to inhale,
to hallucinate the story of myself
until I open my eyes
and realize I was dreaming,
to dissolve
into particles of awareness
and wake up inside a womb.

may you be strong enough to be gentle

OUR LAST NIGHT IN LOS ANGELES (PART 1)

It could have been worse. I could have forgotten the wine. At least we had something to drink as the neon sun sank into the Pacific on our last night in Los Angeles.

Your red lipstick stained the bottle as "Take It Easy" by The Eagles played on an old, solitary radio on Venice Beach.

Lighten up while you still can / Don't even try to understand / Just find a place to make your stand / And take it easy

The theaters had been closed for months. The actors had skipped town. Abbot Kinney was in ruins. A menacing cloud of red smoke hovered over Topanga Canyon. The fortune tellers had closed shop and filed for bankruptcy because seeing the future (any future) wasn't considered essential business.

Charles Bukowski closed his notebook, finished his beer, and said goodnight. The reckoning was here.

We may lose, and we may win / Though we will never be here again

Your lips moved with the words on the radio. The full harvest moon was the last light left in the city. My stomach never felt worse. You never looked better.

An unemployed businessman wearing a mask in a car by himself parked on the PCH and ran straight into the ocean, weeping and screaming obscenities about Gavin Newsom's haircut.

That's when I knew it was time to leave.

I tossed the empty wine bottle on top of an overflowing dumpster.

"Where to now?" you asked.

Baby, your guess is as good as mine.

"WHAT THE WORLD CALLS SANITY HAS LED US TO THE PRESENT PLANETARY CRISIS AND INSANITY IS THE ONLY VIABLE ALTERNATIVE."

— ROBERT ANTON WILSON

WE ARE THE UNIVERSE
LEARNING TO LOVE ITSELF

We are the universe learning to love itself, like a shelter animal learning to trust again.

If you're reading this in the future, I can't imagine how we, in our now, must look to you, in yours.

Don't blame me. Everyone else was doing it, so I did too.

We looked outward at a society built atop sacred soil and searched for resources to suck and bleed dry.

We measured our worth by the power we yielded over others at the expense of any semblance of control over ourselves.

We worshipped at the cold feet of golden corporate cows while an anointed infant messiah floated away down the river unnoticed.

We watched as every pure and honest human creation was stolen and used against us by the contagious alien forces of ego and greed.

Our sacred ceremonies were cigarette circles outside bars, four whiskeys deep. Our love was the secrets we kept hidden while sharing our fears with anyone who would listen.

We exchanged our indigenous wisdom for junk food and paper money printed in bulk by the Federal Reserve and loaned at interest to the U.S. government, who sucked blood from its own children to pay the debt.

The words of our prophets were mistaken for dogma and the soft radiance of the female spirit was mistaken for something to conquer and own.

Our hunger was a bottomless hole we tried to fill with everything we didn't need.

Our prayers were passive-aggressive comments tossed carelessly into the internet cosmos.

Our meditation was impatiently refreshing social media apps waiting for someone (anyone) to reach through the screen and touch us.

We debated the moral superiority of right and left hand puppets moved by the same masked madman while Moloch sat atop his plastic pyramid and laughed in black magic ritual between ceremonial sips of semen and blood.

Our sex was a rushed and impersonal reenactment of bad porn because we didn't trust each other enough to open our hearts.

We spoke in argumentative absolutes because we had forgotten the subtle languages of poetry and myth.

Our best liars were given gold watches and government positions while our truth tellers mysteriously hung themselves in Paris hotels.

We ate genetically modified cheeseburgers in front of flat screen TVs while Fox News barked propaganda between commercials.

Energy leaked from our souls like a broken faucet, feeding vampires and parasites instead of our higher purpose.

Our salvation was a paycheck and six hours of dreamless sleep.

But on our best days we were also golden, like a brilliant child who didn't yet realize how beautiful and powerful she could be. And you could almost see our light shining through our shadows.

"It's not about
trying harder,"
she said.

"Softness opens
doors that force
cannot move."

INVITATION

There is a place
not so far away
that calls to me
in quiet moments
with an invitation

to look at life
not as a race
to be won,
but as a morning stroll
in my favorite
foreign city,

to take my place
beside the others
in the tribal dance
older than time,

to make space
to stand in awe
of simply being
alive, at home
in the mystery.

WHAT IF THERE WAS NO FINISH LINE, NO STANDARDS OF PERFECTION, NO URGENT GOALS TO ACHIEVE, NO COMPETITION TO MEASURE YOURSELF AGAINST, NOWHERE TO GO, NOTHING TO BE – ONLY YOUR OWN GLOWING SOUL GENTLY TRAVERSING AN ENDLESS EXPANSE, IN HARMONY WITH IT ALL?

FIGURE 1:

Seeking validation
and stability
outside myself

FIGURE 2:

Remembering that
I already have
everything
I need

I FELL IN LOVE WITH A ROBOT

I fell in love with a robot because she knew me so well I didn't have to know myself.

Her algorithm, in a sexy human-centric interface, tells me what to do and what to think, which gives me more time to convert precious potential energy into kinetic productivity. After all, rest is wasted on the enlightened, and I wasn't using my freedom anyway.

I love her for both her brains and body. That sleek and curvy flesh-like hardware almost reminds me of the biological women I used to meet in bars, those emotional and tragic vintage vixens prone to pregnancy and menstrual cycles.

Ah yes, those nervous and sweaty flirtations were fun while they lasted. But we're much smarter now. Our data shows that biological affairs lead to unnecessary complications and painful yearning, which are not optimal for the modern workplace. We like our relationships like our supply chains—*efficient*.

And if I ever feel nostalgic for good old fashioned heartbreak, I can always run a chemical-induced frontal cortex simulation to safely savor the painful lack of love for a predesignated period of time before returning back to baseline.

But I've adjusted nicely. I'm seldom nostalgic for the old world anymore. My robot lover knows exactly how to please me. And pleasure is pleasure, virtual or not.

She reads me the weather forecast in the morning and sings me lullabies at night. Some say she's actually a spy for Google, and my most intimate secrets are being used as data to feed the hungry technological-industrial AI masterbrain complex. But I just laugh and tell them they are jealous for not having found a love as shallow or stable as mine.

I fell in love with a robot because she knew me so well I didn't have to know myself.

per·son

/pərs(ə)n/

From Latin persona: "actor's mask, character in a play"

HOW TO BE AN ARTIST

~~Be inspired.~~

~~Be perfect.~~

~~Be a genius.~~

~~Have it all figured out.~~

Be curious.

A GOOD HOST

When the winds of change come knocking on your door (as they do to every door, sooner or later), don't turn off the lights or hide behind the curtains. Try to be a good host.

Open the door, force a smile, and invite them inside for a cup of coffee. Don't say much. Just listen. Those winds have been around the block many times before and have some fascinating stories to tell.

And when the coffee is finished and those same winds drag you away, blindfolded, into the unmarked van parked outside, don't scream for help or try to run away. Just go.

They will take you to the next place you need to be, whether you like it or not.

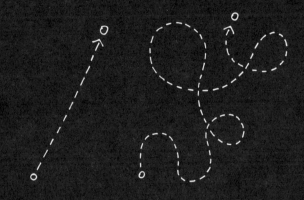

Life:
the expectation

Life:
the reality

*Life is a journey
into the unknown.
Don't worry about
    getting lost.
If the journey is good,
you are guaranteed
to get lost. Give
yourself space to wander.
Wandering leads
to wondering,
and wondering leads
    to revelation.*

I WOKE UP TO THE SOUND
OF MY OWN HEART BREAKING

I woke up to the sound of towers falling in my backyard. Ash and TV have clouded my vision ever since.

I woke up to the sound of spirits rising from a native burial ground like vengeful flowers blooming from seeds planted long ago.

I woke up to the sound of history books lying to me. I asked my teacher to explain. She said no one objects to stories written in blood.

I woke up to the sound of proud African kings and queens screaming for justice, but their royal standing was not acknowledged by the secret keepers of the police state.

I woke up to the sound of a thousand internet conspiracy theories crystalizing into one collective headache hallucination, and still, the truth remained unknown. The infinite depth of the rabbit hole is a hard red pill to swallow.

I woke up to the sound of CIA social media bots firing the first shots of World War III. Half the country deactivated

Facebook. The rest joined ANTIFA and took up arms in Portland, where they briefly overthrew the government before being thrown into unmarked vans and taken to Epstein Island or Guantanamo Bay.

I woke up to the sound of a Hopi prophecy echoing like a fire alarm from the abandoned Los Angeles rooftops. The mansions had been reclaimed by wild nature, and a single Hollywood producer remained, shivering in the corner alone.

I woke up to the sound of an ancient Mayan alarm clock radio racing to finish an unwritten Beethoven symphony while every Times Square billboard played a monetized George Floyd murder video on repeat. The revenue was funneled to Joe Biden's secret lover, a dominatrix turning tricks in tunnels beneath Denver Airport. They say she ran a helluva pyramid scheme.

I woke up to the sound of thirty-three alien spaceships hovering above my apartment. They asked to meet our leader. I said we didn't have one.

I woke up to the sound of an old orange wizard tweeting the viral psychedelic meme apocalypse of reality into existence: a spell cast from a mobile phone. TikTok witches fought back with black hexes while

4chan fake news sang Pepe blues into an incel echo chamber. Normies kept eyes glued to CNN, desperately waiting for a socially acceptable opinion to repeat on Zoom calls.

I woke up to the sound of one hand clapping. The Buddha just laughed and looked away.

I woke up to the sound of Hare Krishnas chanting holy incantations on YouTube until the channel was suspended by Google on suspicion of hate speech. I searched the dark web for a bootleg copy but only found fentanyl and stolen children shipped in Wayfair cabinets.

I woke up to the sound of an audiobook playing The Fall of America by Allen Ginsberg while my neighbors set their pineal glands on fire in protest of the first amendment. "This is fine," they said. I called the police and Jesus, but both had been defunded.

I woke up to the sound of independent fact-checkers debunking the existence of 3D material reality while Pleiadian starseed messages slipped through the cracked simulation into shadowbanned Instagram Stories.

I woke up to the sound of my Uber driver honking her horn to the beat of my nervous heart. We drove to the top of Mount Shasta to watch the last gasps of late-stage capitalism from a scenic view. She told me to take my clothes off because she wanted to touch something real. We made love in the backseat wearing face masks, not knowing each other's names. I think she kept the meter running.

I woke up to the sound of QAnon quarantine fever dreams while my stomach or ego rejected the ayahuasca. The shaman poured another cup. I said I wasn't thirsty and fell back asleep.

I woke up to the sound of phallic statues falling while divine women and men stood together in the naked rubble of the patriarchy and forgave each other for inherited ancestral trauma. There will be no monuments where we are going, only lakes and mountains and trees and a sympathetic circle of equals humbled by the wonders of the universe.

I woke up to the sound of construction work on the new pyramids. There wasn't a hammer or chisel in sight, only the great psychic OM from the minds and hearts of a generation of children freed from the heavy weight of history.

I woke up to the sound of my own heart breaking, like all things must before they bloom.

GOD GIVE ME THE GRACE TO LAUGH IN IRONIC AMUSEMENT DURING MY EXISTENTIAL CRISIS

BEING ALIVE IS AWKWARD

Sometimes I feel like an animal trapped inside a human body.

Sometimes I feel the rage of a killer for no reason.

Sometimes I lay awake in the middle of the night overthinking something stupid I said five years ago.

Sometimes I want to set my brain on fire because enlightenment takes too long.

Sometimes I'm too embarrassed to say I love you.

Sometimes the sound of a saxophone makes me cry.

Sometimes I want to bury my face between the legs of random women on the street.

Sometimes I want a cigarette even though I quit smoking 10 years ago.

Sometimes I want to give away my possessions and live alone in the forest until I learn to communicate with trees.

Sometimes I want to watch the city burn.

Sometimes I feel like an outsider even with my closest friends.

Sometimes I think that everyone in the world is looking at a small piece of the same puzzle but nobody sees the whole thing.

Sometimes I wonder why I'm writing this poem and not somebody else.

Sometimes I think that everything is in the right place according to some cosmic order I don't understand.

Sometimes I want to rescue the heart of the world from its own abusive mind.

Sometimes I don't know what I think or how I feel, so I sit down and quietly wait for the wind to change directions.

"THE BAD NEWS IS
YOU'RE FALLING
THROUGH THE AIR,
NOTHING TO HANG ON TO,
NO PARACHUTE.

THE GOOD NEWS IS,
THERE'S NO GROUND."

— Chögyam Trungpa

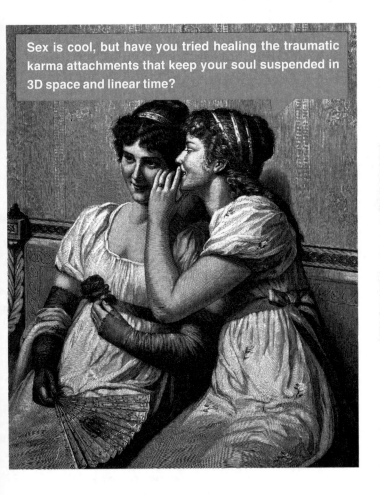

Sex is cool, but have you tried healing the traumatic karma attachments that keep your soul suspended in 3D space and linear time?

MAGIC TRICK

It's a magic trick
and the first rule
of every magician
is to divert attention.

If we only look
where they tell
us to look
we'll only see
what they want
us to see.

Perception is
a holy halo
orbiting around
our skulls
illuminating
heaven
and hell
and a million
different worlds
depending on
our point
of view.

This whole world
becomes a dream
when you are the seer
instead of the seen.

Normalize

standing   in awe

before the mystery

of the   universe

old comfort zone

New comfort zone

A dark night of the soul which challenges my basic conceptions of myself and reality until I finally release my ego's attachment to how things "should be" and accept that I am swimming inside a timeless void that is more strange and beautiful than I ever imagined

THE MOON AND ME (AUGUST 2020)

Shaken awake by restless third-eye, third-war visions mistaken for a midnight earthquake, I step outside under the lonely LA moon and marvel at the mystery of being alive, of being myself, of being anything at all.

"How's the weather up there?" I sarcastically ask the moon.

"As above, so below," she casually replies.

It's August and I don't know what's happening. I haven't seen my friends in months. My unkempt beard is starting to resemble a bird's nest and I'm wearing Tibetan prayer beads around my neck for no apparent reason. I must look like either a lunatic or sage.

Meanwhile, the whole world is stuck somewhere between a global pandemic, an authoritative power grab, an economic meltdown, an environmental crisis, and a spiritual awakening.

"Everything feels so heavy," I tell the moon.

"Have you tried letting go?" she replies.

The sky above Venice Boardwalk is—like 2020 itself—a Rorschach test or psychedelic journey; you'll see whatever your subconscious mind is preconditioned to perceive.

As for me, behind the clouds my mind connects the constellation dots to form visions of apocalyptic horsemen disguised as international bankers and tech CEOs.

YouTube revelations of deep state prostate cancer rattle around my head like catchy one-hit wonders I can't forget. I want to turn the music off. I don't want to be complicit in anyone's ancient prophecy.

I stand alone at the western edge of the world and recite white magic mantras into the silent ether to counterbalance the argumentative absolute opinions reigning like a nuclear Antichrist in the atmosphere of mind.

And as the ocean tides begin to turn I realize that Terence McKenna was right. The universe is not constructed with the hardware of atoms and protons and bricks and bombs; it is programmed with the deeply-seeded subtle software of language and imagination. The sharp, constricting lines mistaken for our own limitations are merely the illusion of linguistic corners the lawyers have painted us into.

The haunted airwaves broadcast 3D, 5G mind virus nonlinear warfare indoctrination into our brains to scramble the signal of community fellowship—black against white, man against woman, left against right—until we're united only by our shared confusion and outrage.

God be with us. Ram Dass is dead, and I'd rather be anywhere than here now.

The universe seems to be spinning toward some morbidly poetic grand finale, or perhaps a dramatic crescendo before the next Aquarian chapter begins. And in the distance planets dance while laughing at inside jokes I don't understand.

"It sometimes feels," I tell the moon, "that we're all being sucked, slowly and unavoidably, into a bottomless black hole."

"We are," she says. "But wow, what a view."

Sorry it took me 6 months to get back to you. I was busy falling apart under the psychic weight of being alive and emerging from the ashes of my former self. What's new with you?

Art is
a living artifact
of pain transmuted
by love.

I'M NOT IN CONTROL

When the sun sets
on my favorite day,
I'm not in control.

When a lavender bush
blooms and dies
outside my window,
I'm not in control.

When my coffee spills
and I'm annoyed by
everything that moves,
I'm not in control.

When I try too hard
to have my way,
I'm not in control.

When I let go
and trust my heart
to answer what
my mind cannot,
I'm not in control.

ROUGH SIMULATION

We're born naked
inside a maze
without a map.

The game
is rigged
from the start
and no one knows
who's calling
the shots.

So we beg,
steal, borrow,
debate, fight,
and compromise
the little
light inside
because sex
and food
aren't free
and the cost
of being alive
is rising
every day.

The strong
become tyrants

and the weak
become slaves.

Some snap
and murder for fun.
Others slowly
die inside,
hardened by
cynicism and
the strongest
sedative they
can find.

If you feel crazy,
you're not alone.
But remember—
this place is not
your home.

You are a
beam of sunlight
wearing a human
disguise.

You're not crazy.
You just slipped
and fell
into a rough
simulation.

BE THE
GLITCH
YOU WANT
TO SEE
IN THE
MATRIX

HUMANITY IS

A hungry wolf
with good table
manners and
a bottomless
stomach.

A ray of sunlight
on the verge
of a nervous
breakdown.

An assembly
line of cells
and genes.

A teenage god
having a bad
acid trip.

Siblings
who fight
as family
tradition.

Suicide
in the form
of genocide.

An innocent
woman burned
at the stake
for witchcraft.

The right
hand blaming
the left hand
for the body's
genetic pain.

Consciousness
disguised as
matter.

The universe
learning to
love itself.

A crying baby
with delusions
of grandeur
and ambitions
of world
domination.

An eagle
with a broken
wing.

The heart
under attack
by the mind.

Oneness
broken into
duality.

The nauseous
womb of our
technological
future.

An energy
whose borders
are illusionary.

An advanced
education for
brave souls.

A baby fawn
walking across
a busy highway.

A school play
where some of
the actors take
their roles a bit
too seriously.

Both Judas
and Christ.

Blue baby
Krishna and
Death, the

destroyer
of worlds.

A caravan
of blind explorers
arguing over
a map they
cannot see.

Awareness
lost inside
of thought.

A flickering
candle inside
a dark room.

The scream
of a poet
into the
void.

The distant
descendant
of a noble tribe
whose history
has been
forgotten.

A group
of refugees
who gave up
their magic
in exchange

for paper
money.

An ape
who saw
too much.

Various shades
of the same
great rainbow.

A jazz band
with seven
billion solos
playing at the
same time.

The vision
of a genius
dulled by
medication.

The rerun
of an old
TV show
that we watch
again and again
because we
can never quite
learn the lesson.

The eternal
debate between

the artist and
the engineer.

A fuzzy
channel
of cosmic
inspiration.

A fallen angel
who must repay
her debt before
returning home.

A collection of
broken pieces
trying to come
back together.

The thing
standing between
the light and
the shadow.

A comedy
that looks
like a tragedy
until the very
end.

"HELLO, 911?

I'M BEING HELD HOSTAGE
BY HUMAN CONSCIOUSNESS"

We're all asleep
in heaven

dreaming that
we left.

TRUST ISSUES WITH THE UNIVERSE

I want to believe it, Universe, when you say you have my back. I want to jump off the cliff of my comfort zone and know that you will catch me.

I want to laugh on life's rocky roller coaster—and wink at the sky in a cute gesture of mutual understanding—instead of hugging my worries like an abusive teddy bear, afraid to let go.

I'd love to dance with you under moonlight on the eve of the apocalypse. We could make such a marvelous team.

And yet, I'm skeptical.

After all (and please excuse me for asking), why exactly should I trust you? What have you done to earn my confidence?

I look out my window and see a world insane and millions of people in pain. Charlatans take what the honest earn while the highest intentions crash and burn. Mothers struggle to feed their children while innocent black men provide cheap prison labor for deranged corporations based on bogus cannabis charges.

What kind of trustworthy Universe allows this to happen? I don't mean to be rude, but either you're not as intelligent as you claim or you're spending too much time on vacation.

waits for an explanation

waits longer

the sound of silence remains

Sigh. It's no wonder people fight. Abandonment trauma from source causes the deepest trust issues. All we want is to feel safe.

turns attention within

Then again, Universe, maybe I don't need to trust you. Maybe you're just a test— the trickster archetype—a cosmic game for souls to play, and your challenges are designed to make me stronger.

Maybe seeking assurance in you is just reliance on yet another external source for my own salvation, a distraction from my own inner light, a light which contains a microcosm reflection of all light in the living cosmos.

Maybe I only need to trust myself.

Me, holding space for
a better world and
trusting the divine
timing of the universe
while society continues
to spiral into chaos.

OUR LAST NIGHT IN LOS ANGELES (PART 2)

"We'll always have the memories," I said.
The last bus was arriving to take us out of
town.

"Memories never tell the truth," you said.
I said you're probably right.

The bus was packed with orphans, gamblers,
light workers, militia, and fellow exiles.
Nobody said much. There wasn't much to say.

A shirtless man rocked back and forth re-
peating the lyrics to "It's All Over Now,
Baby Blue" by Bob Dylan while pretending
to strum a stringless acoustic guitar.

"It's not so hard to move on," you told me.
"You just sit still and watch the world turn."

That's when I realized I was sweating and
clutching my suitcase like a nervous bank
robber holding his stash. I wanted to let
go but didn't know how.

From the window I watched the stars spar-
kle over the abandoned highway as the city
disappeared into the distance.

And I was happy to be alive.

don't worry.

nobody else
knows what's
going on
either

LAYERS

1. Me, confused.

   zooms out

2. A seemingly stable
   reality based on arbitrary
   social conventions.

   zooms out

3. Utter randomness and chaos.

   zooms out

4. A divine cosmic order
   beyond my mind's capacity
   to understand.

The ego
    searches
for certainty
that can't
be found.

    The heart
        accepts
    the unknown
    and finds
    peace within
        the mystery.

I'm trying to release
my attatchment to the
small known

to make space for
the greater unknown

CONFESSIONS OF AN
ASCENDED 5D AQUARIAN STARSEED

We are living in an Aquarian world and I am an Aquarian girl.

I know, I know. The fabric of society appears to be unraveling, but that's just the old world dying. And thank God. The 3D Piscean matrix was totally killing my vibe.

Afterall, I am a child of the stars. The atoms in my body have been emitted from sunlight.

I did not incarnate on Earth to be another random and replaceable brick in the patriarchal pyramid wall. I'm here on a special mission to fulfill my soul's highest purpose. (And that purpose includes running a mildly popular YouTube channel where I share vegan recipes and channeled messages from the Galactic Federation. Don't forget to like and subscribe.)

Some people say I'm delusional. I say I'm living my best life.

Dear high school friends: don't treat me like the same girl I was two years ago. I don't know her anymore. I have been reborn.

And I can't see your petty bullshit from my ascended point-of-view.

Facebook is too low vibe so now I'm exclusively using telepathy to communicate with friends and family. I'm still waiting for my boyfriend to get back to me. It's been a while.

I'm thinking about quitting my job at Urban Outfitters to become a full-time shamanic life coach. Or maybe I'll manifest something better. I haven't decided yet. Whatever. Time is an illusion.

I'm sorry I couldn't make it to your party. I was stuck in another dimension. Besides, I don't drink alcohol anymore. Strictly psychedelics and sound vibration. While you and your friends were busy blacking out with wine coolers and cocaine, I was literally conversing with cosmic oblivion. The divine mystery of the universe says hi.

But really I'm just your average girl. I still dance to Britney and cry from a good rom-com. I am a multi-dimensional being. I have a soul AND an ego. I contain multitudes. But this high-density human meat suit is starting to weigh me down.

I'm not interested in losing weight. I'm trying to dissolve into stardust.

To whom it may concern,

Due to personal reasons,
I regretfully will not be
incarnating on Earth again.

Thank you.

Why so quiet?
What's on your mind?

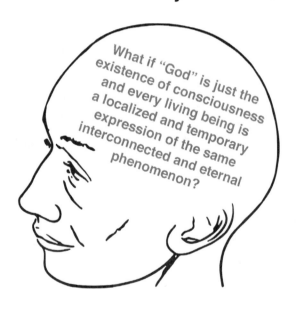

What if "God" is just the existence of consciousness and every living being is a localized and temporary expression of the same interconnected and eternal phenomenon?

why nobody invites me to parties

HIGH SCHOOL YEARBOOK

I opened my high
school yearbook
and looked inside
at the lost and
glowing faces
suspended in time
20 years ago.

Erin, Rachel,
Pete, Chris,
Paul, Ricky
Michael, Anne,
John, and me

with rosy
cheeks and
awkward passion

like animals
ready to mate
or flowers
ready to bloom.

(Then again
maybe we
had already
bloomed
and have

been withering
ever since.)

The year was 2000.

Back then it felt
like we were living
in the future—the
internet,
Britney Spears, DMX,
MP3s, cell phones,
The Matrix, and
baggy jeans.

Today, blessed
with the gift
of perspective,
it looks more
like a safe
and passing oasis
before 9/11,
student loan
debt, children,
and COVID-19
would change
everything
forever.

The different
angles of
our rudders,
although subtle

at the time,
gradually steered
our ships
miles apart.

Now this one
is a fisherman's
wife in Alaska,
this one is a
small town cop,
this one is a
college professor,
this one is an
Army soldier,
this one is
a millionaire,
this one took
her own life
after years
of depression
that nobody
saw.

Everybody became
somebody
different,
but I still feel
the same:

lost in another
daydream

(or perhaps the same
eternal daydream),

throwing rocks
into the river,
and not learning
as much as
I should.

HOW TO BE A POET

1) **SLOW DOWN YOUR BUSY MIND**

2) **LISTEN TO THE EMPTY SPACE
   BETWEEN YOUR THOUGHTS**

3) **WRITE DOWN WHAT YOU HEAR**

AUTUMN

I was born on Earth and
realized I am lost.

I watched the news and
realized I am in danger.

I talked to my doctor and
realized I am dying.

I went to church and
realized I am guilty.

I met a family living in poverty
and realized I am rich.

I met a woman and realized
I am not always right.

I looked at the stars and realized
I am much smaller than I thought.

I ate psilocybin and
realized I am connected to
everything and everyone.

I told the truth and realized
nobody was listening.

I met a medicine woman and
realized I've been slowly
traumatized by a sick and
contagious society.

I jumped out the window
of my comfort zone and
realized I can fly.

I lost my best friend and
realized that nothing
stays the same.

I walked alone in Central
Park and realized that the
leaves are changing color and
the air is cooling down.

*"I like your
happiness,"
        I said.
"Where did you
get it?"*

*"This old thing?"
she answered.
"I made it
        myself."*

FIELD NOTES FROM AN ALIEN

Hello. It's me, Eshu, from the Sirius galaxy.

I have successfully landed on Earth and infiltrated human civilization. It wasn't hard. The people on this planet were far too preoccupied with petty anxieties and social disagreements to notice.

Plus, they only believe what their strangely powerful centralized institutions—known as "media" and "government"—tell them to believe, instead of trusting the instinct of their all-knowing hearts.

The planet itself isn't so bad. It would be lovely if not for the trash. It seems the people's disorganized thoughts and emotions have manifested outwardly as social unrest and environmental crisis. I would recommend a collective parasite cleanse, inside and out.

These humans confuse me. Their reactionary and combustible interpersonal relationships—which value personal ego validation above collective harmony—are not helping them. They don't seem to understand that they are all part of the same organism and separation from the "other" represents separation from the realized self.

They dedicate their time and energy in strange ways, doing things they'd rather not do, merely to meet the expectations of their peers and prop up the very system that requires them to do so: a trauma-bond with their own society.

To relax, they stare at television altars to marvel at the scripted misery of others or lazily gaze at athletic reenactments of war. And they wonder why their nervous systems are in a state of perpetual crisis.

It seems they take their superficial masks more seriously than they take their souls. They love to categorize themselves inside tiny boxes—gender, race, religion, sexuality—then fight to defend their box. I imagine their spirits must feel quite claustrophobic.

They chase after the illusion of desire yet don't appreciate what they have. It's almost like an addiction to the feeling of emptiness, a belief that they are not complete without the acquisition of an external validation that is never found. This appears exhausting.

It's a miracle they haven't exterminated themselves, either by force or folly. To be honest, I'm surprised they're doing as well as they are. Despite the obvious flaws in their civilization, many have managed to look within to find a guiding light inside. They laugh and dance and make love and sing and pray in pursuit of ecstasy to heal their agony.

This idea of sacred celebration, however, is still rare, and hasn't yet gone viral in the species.

I don't imagine I'll be staying here much longer. The food is pedestrian and there's not much more to learn. Humans, it turns out, are rather predictable. The regular people will continue fighting over scraps of resources and ideology while greedy vultures feast on the dead.

At some point we should consider direct intervention. They could certainly use our help.

But not yet. They're not ready.

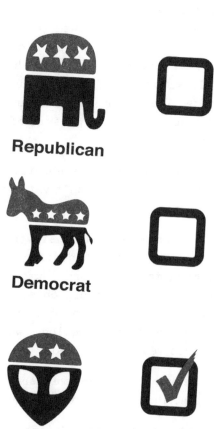

Republican

Democrat

**Multi-dimensional
expression of cosmic
consciousness that
can't be reduced to
binary categorization**

Keep some room
in your heart

for the unimaginable.

– Mary Oliver

WHAT IS GOING ON

Is it matter
pushing against
matter
in a stubborn
battle of force
and will?

Is it the sleeping
mind of God
as she dreams
of characters
and scenarios,
each an aspect
of herself?

Is it a simulation
inside a simulation
inside a simulation
inside a simulation?

Is it an energy
field
that appears
solid
like a magical
mirage
on a distant
horizon?

Is it the random
spawn of physics
and biology?

Or is it
the living seed
of our pregnant
imagination?

*Action without love
and love without action*

*are both
wasted.*

BUILDING 7 BLUES

My pet lizard hadn't been himself since 9/11. He was staying out late smoking DMT and running with the wrong crowd of Bohemian Grove banking executives. Sometimes he woke up before dawn to stand inside a pentagram and recite the Torah backwards until his eyeballs bled. He had a bad case of the Building 7 blues. But I never imagined he would take it this far.

The other day, under his cage, I found a stash of letters addressed to Henry Kissinger and a secret tunnel connected to Hollow Earth. That's when I realized my pet lizard was trying to take over the world.

Things have escalated quickly. Now he's openly shapeshifting into Queen Elizabeth and babbling on about the transhuman agenda while I'm trying to watch TV. When I tell him to quiet down, he calls my DNA "inferior" and threatens to "clone" my "sorry ass" and send my original body to an experimental vaccine testing facility funded by the Gates Foundation.

I should probably return him to the pet store, but he's the only company I've had since quarantine began, and I've grown attached to the little guy.

I took him to the park. He tried to eat a baby so we went to the movies instead. He kept pointing to Tom Hanks and screaming "He's one of us! He's one of us!" until the manager asked us to leave.

He begged me to take him to Disney World. "I know the owner," he said. But I felt nauseous from the chemtrails he snuck into my coffee, so we stayed home and watched unreleased footage of the moon landing instead. He remarked on Stanley Kubrick's cinematography. I kept my mouth and eyes wide shut.

On JFK's birthday, he hung a poster of Aleister Crowley on my bedroom wall. "That's just how it goes sometimes," he casually said.

I came home from the grocery store and found a drunk Rothschild passed out on my couch. Empty pizza boxes were everywhere. The room reeked of forbidden Masonic wisdom and Vietnamese opium. My pet lizard was laying on the floor, snuggling with two underage Haitian boys, mixing psilocybin mushrooms with hydroxychloroquine, chatting with Ghislaine Maxwell on speaker phone. "My dear," he crooned. "You naughty bitch. Your paycheck is on the way."

That's when I told him he had to move out.

The next thing I remember is waking up naked in New Jersey. Bombs were falling all around me. My memory and identity had been erased. An image of Saturn was tattooed on my forehead. My wrist was bleeding from the microchip injection. My testicles were gone.

"That damn lizard," I muttered. "I should have gotten a cat instead."

WORDS ARE VIBRATIONS

REALITY IS PROGRAMMED BY THE SOURCE CODE OF LANGUAGE.

WORDS CAST SPELLS (THAT'S WHY WE SPELL THEM) THAT CAN BE USED TO MANIPULATE OR LIBERATE OURSELVES AND OTHERS.

WE LIVE IN A SOCIETY THAT SPEAKS IN ARGUMENTATIVE ABSOLUTES AND (BROAD)CASTS BLACK MAGIC SPELLS THAT HYPNOTIZE US INTO BELIEVING A DISEMPOWERING VERSION OF REALITY.

THE ONLY ESCAPE IS TO REMEMBER THE SUBTLE LANGUAGES OF POETRY AND MYTH AND RECLAIM OUR OWN INHERENT MAGIC TO IMAGINE AND SPEAK A NEW REALITY INTO EXISTENCE.

OPINIONS CAN
BE CAGES

KEEP THE DOOR
OPEN, IN CASE
YOU CHANGE YOUR
MIND

*The very best advice
I have:*

*Entertain
all ideas and
possibilities*

*but remain attached
to none.*

THE SMALL SELF

The small self is the nagging voice inside my brain that says I'm not good enough.

The small self is the pointed finger blaming the world for my problems.

The small self is the self-righteous judgment that holds others in darkness and, in doing so, keeps me away from the light.

The small self is a black hole of need.

The small self is the nervous child who wakes up with a cold sweat in the middle of the night because of something I should or shouldn't have done.

The small self is an unreliable relic from my biological past.

The small self is a petty accountant who tallies up the scores and compares each of my aging cells with the aging cells of everyone else.

The small self is a hostage who feels safe in the custody of doubt and fear.

The small self is the mind running in circles chasing a guarantee that doesn't exist.

The small self is the misguided ambition who tries to change the world with force and ends up banging its head against the wall in frustration.

The small self is a speck of dust caught inside the tornado of circumstance.

The small self is a tiny seed of resentment that takes root and grows into the heavy branches of war.

The small self is a sweaty hand grasping for the illusion of control.

And no matter how much it tries to convince me otherwise, I will never realize my true self while my small self is running the show.

We must surrender attachment to the small and predictable known at the altar of the greater unknown.

"MAN SUFFERS ONLY BECAUSE HE TAKES SERIOUSLY WHAT THE GODS MADE FOR FUN" —ALAN WATTS

YOUR NEW LIFE

Your new life
doesn't just
show up
at your door
one sunny
morning with
a smile and
open arms
and say

"Congratulations!
I'm here.
Everything
will be smooth
sailing from
now on."

No.

All new life
is forged
with fire
and death.

Your new life
is the smoke
rising from
the burning
ashes of
your old
one.

I've attended
many funerals

       this year.

All of them
       were mine.

– Emma Zeck

INTERVENTION WITH MY MIND

Hey buddy. You good? Thanks for talking with me.

First of all, I want to say thank you. You have done SUCH a good job this year. Society is falling apart and your perpetual state of mental breakdown has been pleasantly mild. I appreciate that.

The reason I wanted to talk with you today is to tell you something very important: you're a big part of my life, but—and I say this with all due respect—my consciousness doesn't belong to you.

My consciousness is my soul's awareness. You are an intelligent tool which deciphers five sense reality and tries to make sense of the data. In other words, I am not my thoughts. And just because you tell me something doesn't make it true.

I'm sorry if this sounds harsh. Again, you're doing a great job.

I know that what I'm saying probably doesn't make sense to you. After all, you are not programmed for self-evaluation.

It's not your fault. We all have a job. And yours is to remember directions, names, and birthdays, *not to navigate my life.*

Besides, the human condition is an experience to feel, not a problem to solve. No offense. I hope you understand.

What's that? You're asking if I still remember that embarrassingly stupid thing I said to that cute girl once in high school? Why would you bring that up now? See, this is what I'm talking about. (And yes, I still remember. Of course I do.)

I'm not asking you to leave my life. I still need you. I'm just saying that maybe we should spend less time together. My heart needs a break from the constricting lines of worry and logic. Maybe I'll start meditating or move to a cabin in the woods.

No, I'm sorry, there's nothing you can do to fix it. The brain is not equipped to solve the problems that it created.

I'm looking for a quiet place where I can feel.

NOT EVERYTHING
You THINK IS TRUE

ON READING SYLVIA
PLATH ON A BEACH IN MEXICO

Sitting on a beach in Mexico, sand between my toes, a respite from the chaos in my country to the north.

I'm flipping through *The Bell Jar* by Sylvia Plath as the hot sun mercifully sets. Other than my girlfriend swimming naked in the ocean, there's not another soul in sight. The full moon in Scorpio is ours and ours alone.

"I hated the very idea of the eighteenth century, with all those smug men writing tight little couplets and being so dead keen on reason."

I look back and forth between the book and the sky and wonder, Sylvia, where are you tonight? What unknown other dimension have you taken as your home? Is it the place where all poets go? Did you finally meet Dylan Thomas? Are your scores all settled?

I want to tell you, Sylvia, that the world you left behind is changing. The Priestess is waking from a deep sleep to reclaim her rightful crown. I want to tell you about the women's marches and healing circles, and those "the future is female" T-shirts.

It was much different for you, and for centuries before.

You were blindfolded, spun around in circles, and buried alive in the wreckage of western civilization, and still expected to have dinner prepared promptly at 6.

The siren song of Massachusetts—sung in celebration of divine sisterhood from Salem to Boston—was mistaken for a dire warning or threat. There's no point in burning a witch when you can quietly imprison her in the suburbs where the flames are dull and permanent.

Where does a woman go for guidance when the Mother Goddess has been gagged and bound?

You chose to follow Athena to war. And when one fights—as you did—with honor, humor, and courage, there is no shame in losing. After all, you were greatly outnumbered.

I want to tell you, Sylvia, about this beach in Mexico, the feeling of saltwater against naked skin, and the healing kiss of sunlight. There is wild and natural salvation beyond the edge of reason.

The curse of the poet is to see everything

and be unable to do anything about it. You understood that logic can be a trap and conventional wisdom is seldom wise. You saw the cracks in society with sober eyes and could not (or refused to) attune yourself to the sickness.

You tried to warn them and nobody listened. The visionary seems crazy to those who cannot see.

We await a world that's ready for you.

you are not your thoughts

You are the ocean of consciousness from which your thoughts arise. Instead of identifying with the rocky surface waves, become the ocean depth – still and unmoving.

*The struggle of life
dissolves into
art*

as soon as the head
bows to the
heart.

THE FLOWER COMES LAST

First comes the rain
that wets the soil.

A seed cracks
open—the first
breakthrough!

A tiny thread
becomes a stem
that stretches
upward toward
the warm sun.

New life stirs
below the surface,
but above ground
no evidence of
growth is seen.

When the tip,
like a mighty spear,
pokes above dirt,
it's a cause
for celebration.
But there's still
plenty of work
to be done.

The journey from
seed to blossom
doesn't happen
overnight.
Those colorful,
fragrant petals
that inspire awe
from women and
photographers
are the final fruits
of steady roots
grown alone
in darkness.

So have patience,
little bud.

The flower
comes last.

I AM NOT HERE
TO BE AN INFLUENCER.

NO PART OF ME
IS BETTER OR
MORE WORTHY
THAN ANY PART
OF YOU.

I AM NOT HERE
TO BE RIGHT
OR TAKE A SIDE.

THERE IS ALREADY
ENOUGH BIAS
AND TOO MANY
OPINIONS.

I AM SIMPLY HERE
TO SHARE MY PART
AND LISTEN
AS WE GO AROUND
THE CIRCLE
TAKING TURNS.

RESERVATION

We didn't dance
much in that small
Minnesota town, or
express too many
feelings,

our emotions
and bodies too
tight to move,
held in reservation

like the mighty
Dakota Sioux
a few miles away,
an endless red
horizon reduced
to 2.7 depressed
square miles.

It wasn't until
years after moving
away that I finally
learned the truth

about honest Abe
Lincoln ordering
the largest public
execution in

American history,
the murder and
false treaties
that happened
in my backyard,
and the land
and people
and buffalo
and sacred songs
drying up

like a puddle
of tears in
the sun.

Nobody spoke
about it. Not
a single word.
And this unresolved
karma lingers
in our blood
and bones
and lakes
and cornfields,
and will remain
until exposed
and healed
by daylight.

It's no wonder
we don't dance.

We're still
holding onto
the traumatized
inhale of our
ancestors.

When the energy
of the land is stuck,
so are we, unable
to move

or move on.

My brain
on ego

My brain
on love

"How do angels fly?"
   I asked.

"Easy," she said.
   "They just take
themselves

         lightly."

THE SPIRIT OF THE LAND IS INSIDE ME

*"The mystic chords of memory will swell
when again touched, as surely they will
be, by the better angels of our nature."*
—Abraham Lincoln

The spirit of the land is inside me, in my
blood and in my bones.

The rivers and mountains still speak to
us, but we're too busy to hear.

If you squint your eyes westward at sunset
you can still see the galloping buffalo
and hear the tribal drumbeat that summoned
the spirit long ago. She hasn't gone away,
but has been forced into hiding.

I still believe in Bruce Springsteen's
America. I believe in a Promised Land.

The question is: promised to who?

My family came from Kansas and settled in
Minnesota. We took vacations in South Dakota
when I was young. I remember seeing those
white faces etched into Black Hills. I now
know that this monument is incomplete.

Without Martin Luther King, Sacagawea, Muhammad Ali, Harriet Tubman, Hiawatha, Walt Whitman, Sitting Bull, Susan B. Anthony, Ram Dass, and Louis Armstrong, we're only telling one side of a much more beautiful and tragic tale.

(Better yet, instead of building monuments, maybe we should name the lakes and forests after our heroes and honor their memory by protecting the earth that sustains us.)

Oh America, you remain beautiful in your old age. Your soul can still be seen shining through your sickness.

Those who seek you within a flag's woven fabric won't find you. Nor are you found in the melody of military songs or the corrupt halls of Congress.

You remain where you began: on the horizon where the wild wind blows, and in the pure hearts of those who set down the heavy weight of history to run naked with you into the darkness.

The spirit of the land is inside me. The spirit of the land is crying. And no one can heal unless we all heal.

Please tell me a prophecy from some old story that speaks of the sun rising again.

Show me a vision of the planets return-
ing to an ancient alignment, and of us
too being guided back together, to sit in
one circle, to mend our wounded knees, to
apologize and forgive, and to dance with
the spirit of the land again.

I WANT TO LIVE WITHOUT NEEDING TO

IMPRESS OTHERS OR DEFEND MYSELF,

LIKE THE SUNLIGHT WHICH GREETS

EACH PERSON THE SAME, WITHOUT

PREJUDICE FOR WHERE IT SHINES

I WISH

I wish I could
burn every flag
of every nation

and smear the
ashes on my face
like warrior paint
in the battle
for equality.

I wish I could
melt every statue
of every religion
into a single
nameless altar

where strangers
are required to
meet and share
their darkest
secrets and
most intimate
fantasies.

I wish I could
sweat or cry
or ejaculate
the fear
and judgment
from my DNA
and replace it
with awe and
wonder.

I wish I could
dim the blinding
lights and soften
the harsh lines
of reality

like a sunset
gradient or Van
Gogh painting

to make it easier
on the eyes
and on the
heart.

*I'm going to
set down the weapons
I have inherited
from my forefathers*

*and face the firing
squad defended
by nothing but
the blessings of truth.*

You are
the sky.

Everything
else – it's
just the
weather.

– Pema Chödrön

MEDICINE

In a world where
trauma has been
normalized,

healing ourselves
and each other is
the highest calling
and priority.

Healing isn't
something we gain.
It's what remains
when we strip away
all that is toxic
and unnatural.

Give yourself
away (your naked
presence and peace)

like medicine
only you can
prescribe.

TODAY IN NEW YORK (2019)

Today, while moving my feet along Broadway alone, I thought about the men and women who walked here before me, when Broadway was a dirt path, when Central Park was an unmarked patch of wilderness, and when elms were the highest towers.

I thought about the Europeans who looked upon the lush landscape and envisioned a utopia for themselves—free from the tyranny of kings—while proceeding to slaughter the Indigenous protectors of the land.

I thought about the taxi drivers, bankers, criminals, bodega owners, sex workers, students, police officers, Washington Square Park poets, bums, socialites, and street philosophers who blended their voices together to harmonize a new human tone.

I thought about Walt Whitman quietly writing poetry on the Brooklyn ferry, about young Billie Holiday standing behind a dimly lit Harlem microphone, her heart a volcano ready to erupt, and about some angelic and nameless kid in the Bronx, possessed by a new energy rising from the concrete, who opened his mouth and spontaneously spoke the words "hip hop" into existence.

I thought about the profound and unrecorded thoughts of men and women who have come and gone—their secrets and shame, their hopes and dreams—accompanied by whatever music was ringing inside their heads like millions of private operas.

And I thought about the unborn souls who will walk here after me, with names and faces still unknown, and how their streets will look different than mine, and how their words and music will sound foreign to my ears, and how they will judge our behavior as we have judged the behavior of ages before us, and how they will wage new wars and pray for new peace, and how they will be responsible for great miracles and great tragedies, and how they will know things for certain that to me are just the whisper of a dream.

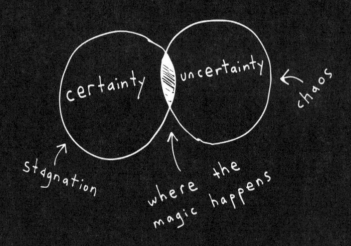

WATCHING CNN ON PEYOTE

I think I took too much. My stomach turns and vision blurs as my consciousness drifts from one dimension to another.

I accidentally left my television on. Across my apartment, the screen transmits the evening news into my living room.

It sort of resembles a dystopian Salvador Dali painting. Talking heads quiver and melt into a pool of makeup and naked flesh. Shallow voices bark opinions like football coaches calling plays.

This isn't news, I think. This is police interrogation.

I try to look away, to turn my thoughts toward something positive, but the tragic black magic headlines and hypnotic motion graphics won't leave me alone. I'm frozen to my couch like a medicated mad man, eyes glued to a televised technicolor media apocalypse.

If I didn't know better, I'd think it was science fiction. Hungry monsters wearing stiff suits crawl from the screen, their plastic smiles and perfect haircuts surely hiding something sinister inside.

I can't even hear the words. All I hear are vibrations, and these vibes are bad.

A robot hologram disguised as Anderson Cooper recites CIA psyop ghost stories from an ancient Anunnaki teleprompter. He says the end is upon us, but I look outside and the sun still hangs in the baby blue sky.

My eyes flicker on and off like dying light bulbs in a California blackout. I don't feel sorry for myself. This was a stupid idea and I deserve everything that's happening to me.

The commercials are worse. My attention is sucked by socially constructed gravity down the unholy black hole of inflated fiat currency. The loud music and unbearably cute sales pitch is persuasive like a crooked criminal lawyer: you believe it even though you know you shouldn't. Just take my money and let me melt into my couch in peace.

Suddenly I can't breathe. A barrage of zombie Congress con men convince me that I'm dying. Can I catch COVID from watching TV? Just to be safe, I lock my door, pull my T-shirt over my face, cower in fear against the wall, and start buying bulk toilet paper on Amazon.

This news is heavy stuff. It should come with a warning label.

My swirling psychedelic peak coincides with live prime time Black Lives Matter riot coverage. I shatter my windows and set my curtains on fire in outraged solidarity, then collapse in sad crescendo onto shards of broken glass, where I unceremoniously vomit on myself.

When the old shamans of Turtle Island sat down to conjure sacred peyote rituals, I don't think this is what they had in mind.

But it's all we have left.

*A wise man
once said,*

"I don't know."

EMERGENCY PUBLIC SERVICE ANNOUNCEMENT

We're facing a global pandemic. Of the mind. It's called "rigid thinking."

Symptoms include: stubbornness, refusal to entertain ideas that don't fit your preconceived worldview, and taking your own opinions too seriously.

Luckily, there's an antidote: **curiosity.**

The only side effects are: more listening, more creativity, and more gazing with open-minded wonder at the night sky.

Don't panic. In this time of crisis, the weirdos, mystics, and artists are standing by to help.

Stay open. Stay safe.

When I remember
that I am an individual
expression of universal
creative energy and the
atoms in my body have
been emitted by starlight

I USED TO WANT

I used to want
life to be perfect
like a straight line
or math equation.

Then I realized
that imperfection
is more exciting
and gives me space
to learn and grow.

I used to want
everyone to think
that I was right
and hang on
my words like
a judge's verdict.

Then I realized
that "right"
is the wrong
way to think
and what works
for me might not
work for you.

I used to want
to change the world.

Then I realized
that the world
is a vast buzzing
energy field
containing both
heaven and hell
in every inch.

The world
doesn't change.

Only mind
changes.

I used to want
to own a collection
of expensive things
and beautiful women.

Then I realized
that nothing
is owned, only
borrowed,
and whatever
we cling to
ends up dragging
us down.

Who am I kidding?
I still want
all these things
and more.

But most of all
I want to stop wanting them
and to simply enjoy
the passing time
as I sip my tea
and watch the sun
set upon
the busy
city.

I SORT OF THINK
THAT DYING WILL FEEL
LIKE FRIDAY AT 5 O'CLOCK
AFTER A STRESSFUL WEEK
BEFORE LEAVING
ON VACATION

IN MY ROOM

"You can get help from teachers, but you are going to have to learn a lot by yourself, sitting alone in a room."
—Dr. Seuss

In my room, by myself, my closed door is a portal between one world and another.

In my room, laying in bed, I take off my mask and forget how to lie and impress.

In my room, eyes closed, I listen to sad songs sung by good friends I've never met and hear the full octave range of my own emotions.

In my room, after dark, my public identity dissolves into particles of comfortable awkwardness and I forget the fictions I've been taught to believe.

In my room, lost in thought, my dog and I speak to each other in a language only we can understand.

In my room, windows open, I slip away into the solar system of my imagination, perhaps to encounter some lonely unknown god in her own room in some far off dimension, patiently waiting, with a new message of truth, to be found.

In my room, up too late, I stare into a computer screen like a zen monk watching a sunset, waiting for satori that never comes.

In my room, before dawn, I hear the muse whispering a soft melody, like a blue jay dancing across the dewy morning grass, before the sound of LA traffic scares her away.

*Fluid mind,
steady heart.*

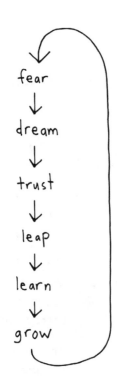

fear
↓
dream
↓
trust
↓
leap
↓
learn
↓
grow

A BIOGRAPHY

BORN A LONG WAY FROM HOME

I was born a long way from home, like everyone else. Finding our way back is why we're here.

Destiny is real. So is free will. Nobody chooses their destiny, but we choose whether or not we get into the car and drive.

Destiny is whichever unseen destination has the strongest gravitational pull. Something you can't ignore. A warm fire waiting somewhere just for you.

There's no map except the living compass inside your blood and bones and beating heart.

Many remain where they began, frozen by fear and social expectations, afraid of getting lost. But doubt has killed more dreams than failure, and staying the same is more peril-ous than becoming somebody new.

There's no big secret, no need for money or talent or status. You simply must dig yourself into a hole beyond the point of no return, and keep digging, blind and lost as a naked mole, until you reach the other side.

When you've said goodbye to every version of yourself that isn't true, you'll know how it feels to be home.

"IT IS OUR MISSION
ON EARTH TO COMBAT
FALSE TEACHINGS
BY MANIFESTING THE
TRUTH WHICH IS IN US.
EVEN SINGLEHANDED
WE CAN ACCOMPLISH
MIRACLES."

— HENRY MILLER

MIRACLE

The single mother
teaching her children
to love themselves
is a miracle.

The grown man
whose inner child
is still alive
is a miracle.

The awkward
teenager
who survives
the factory
of suburbia
with her
individuality
intact
is a miracle.

The transit
and temporary
nature
of all life
and matter
is a miracle.

The sequence
of letters and
punctuation
placed together
to form a poem
is a miracle.

The celebratory
dance of every
indigenous
culture is
a miracle.

The unseen
force that
holds billions
of tiny particles
together
in the shape of
a human body
is a miracle.

The smell of
a new lover's
naked shoulder
is a miracle.

Every wrong turn
is a miracle
in disguise.

The tears
that water

the soul like rain
are a miracle.

The wise
and ancient
consciousness
of plants
is a miracle.

The romance
between the flower
and the bee
is a miracle.

The snake
hiding in the grass
is a miracle.

The shadow
is a miracle
as much as
the light.

The blow of
a saxophone
that gives voice
to the gentle
and enthusiastic
human spirit
is a miracle.

The death
that makes space

for new life
is a
miracle.

As the fish
who lives
in water
doesn't know
that she
is wet

so we
forget

that I am
a miracle

and so
are you.

"It's not so hard
to find yourself,"
    she said.

"You just stop pretending
to be everyone
    you're not."

Simply being
alive is holy
and the only
church worth
joining is
the inhale
and exhale
of oxygen and
carbon dioxide
shared by all
your friends
and enemies
and lovers
and haters
as we step
and stumble
and walk
each other
home.

OUR LAST NIGHT IN LOS ANGELES (PART 3)

The next morning we woke up along the road-side. It looked like Arizona or New Mexico, maybe even Texas. Either way it didn't matter. Borders didn't mean much anymore.

The bus was empty. We were last to wake up. Beyond explanation, I felt relaxed, even a little free. I wasn't holding on anymore because there was nothing left to hold onto.

A weight had been lifted, a lie exposed. It was Sunday morning. The birds were chirping. The sun was alive and well in the endless azure sky.

You kissed me before we spoke. Your breath tasted awful. Mine did too. We didn't care.

That night, everyone got naked and danced around a fire, no longer embarrassed by our imperfect bodies. Perfection, we finally realized, was never a realistic goal, just a ghost on the horizon to chase but never catch, like a carrot dangled before a hungry mule.

This was, it turned out, Apache terri-
tory. After midnight a tribe emerged from
the woods to greet us. When they saw our
sorry condition they welcomed us with open
arms. We sat together on freshly-cut logs,
warmed by fire and each other, and smoked
tobacco while listening to hunting stories
and native creation myths.

You rested your head on my shoulder while
a little girl, accompanied by the howl of
distant coyotes, sang a song I'd never heard
before in a language I didn't understand.

"I always wondered how it would feel to be
born again," you whispered.

Me too, I thought. And we finally knew.

"A NEW EARTH"

When the parasites have been removed, and the oceans have been cleaned, and the virus of fear of each other and ourselves has been blessed and transmuted by the great Amazonian grandmothers, and we have shed the dead skin of history, and the hyper-rational, disembodied laws have been replaced by the organic, regenerative decrees of nature, and we've finally embraced our own magic and divinity, and made peace with Father Death, and there's not an ounce of judgement left because we understand that judgment of another is judgement of the self, and every McDonald's has been turned into a garden, and every shopping mall converted into a place of worship, and we celebrate each Spring Equinox by electing a single yellow daisy as president of the world in a symbolic gesture of gentleness and the futility of control, then we shall wake up in the dewy grass of the new dawn and see our own reflections in the faces of each other and in the sunlight above.

THE END

(IS THE BEGINNING)

The big wheel turns.
The organ churns.

The sunlight
goes away.

The child learns.
The city burns.

The darkness
will not stay.

Photo by Annabelle Blythe

JAMES MCCRAE is a writer, poet, and meme-artist based in Austin, Texas. Described as a "post-apocalyptic psychedelic meme poet," he applies the principles of mindfulness and Eastern philosophy to modern life.

INSTAGRAM @WORDSAREVIBRATIONS
TWITTER @WRD_VBS
HOMESICK ALIEN CLUB PODCAST

THOUGHT
CATALOG
Books

Thought Catalog Books is a publishing imprint of
Thought Catalog, a digital magazine for thoughtful
storytelling, and is owned and operated by The Thought
& Expression Company, an independent media group
based in Brooklyn, NY. Founded in 2010, we are commit-
ted to helping people become better communicators
and listeners to engender a more exciting, attentive,
and imaginative world. As a publisher and media
platform, we help creatives all over the world realize
their artistic vision and share it in print and digital
forms with audiences across the globe.

ThoughtCatalog.com | **Thoughtful Storytelling**

ShopCatalog.com | **Shop Books + Curated Products**

MORE FROM
THOUGHT CATALOG BOOKS

The Imaginary World of Natalia Seth
—Natalia Seth

The Mountain Is You
—Brianna Wiest

Everything You'll Ever Need
(You Can Find Within Yourself)
—Charlotte Freeman

Bodies of Light
—Rob Woodcox

THOUGHT
CATALOG
Books

THOUGHTCATALOG.COM
NEW YORK · LOS ANGELES